# BREAKING THE GENERATIONAL CURSE

LAMONT WILLIAMS

**Written by: Lamont Williams**

Transcribe by: Tina Perry

Edited by: April Smiley

# BREAKING THE GENERATIONAL CURSE

MOCY PUBLISHING, LLC

Detroit, Michigan

BREAKING THE GENERATIONAL CURSE
ISBN 978-0-9834700-4-5
Copyright © 2013 by Lamont Williams

Published by Mocy Publishing, LLC.
Website: www.mocypublishing.com
Email: info@mocypublishing.com
Phone: (313) 436-6944

All rights reserved. Except as permitted under the United States Copyright Act of 1976, no part of this publication may be reproduced or distributed in any form or by any means, or stored in a data base or retrieval system, without the prior written permission of the publisher.

# CONTENTS

| | |
|---|---|
| **ACKNOWLEDGMENTS** | **7** |
| **INTRODUCTION** | **8** |
| CHAPTER 1. **DESCRIBING THE CURSE** | 11 |
| CHAPTER 2. **THE LACK OF EDUCATION** | 14 |
|     THE BLAME GAME | 17 |
|     THE POTENTIAL | 19 |
|     NO RESPECT OF PERSON | 23 |
| CHAPTER 3. **NO ONE SAID IT WOULD BE EASY** | 25 |
| CHAPTER 4. **EVOLVING IN LIFE** | 31 |
|     ONLY DOING WHAT THEY KNOW | 33 |
|     THE LIFE STYLE | 38 |
|     FEAR OF STEPPING OUT THE BOX | 43 |
| CHAPTER 5. **MY LIFE EXPERIENCE** | 47 |
|     IDENTIFYING THE CURSE | 57 |
|     BREAKING THE CURSE | 61 |
| CHAPTER 6. **TRANSFORMATION OF THE MIND** | 64 |
| CHAPTER 7. **BREAKING FREE** | 70 |
|     REACHING BACK | 74 |

| | | | |
|---|---|---|---|
| CHAPTER | 8. | **THE NEW BEGINNING** | **76** |
| CHAPTER | 9. | **THE NEXT GENERATION** | **80** |
| | | CHANGING THE FUTURE | 84 |
| CHAPTER | 10. | **TAKING YOUR LIFE BACK** | **87** |

## ACKNOWLEDGMENTS

I would like to give special Thanks to my cousin/brother, Donele "Casino" Bailey and the rest of my family and friends for inspiring me to write this book. I Thank God who is the head of my life, for always being there for me, and helping me to see and understand the struggles in my life have caused me to grow in many ways, and has enabled me to be instrumental in the lives of many.

## INTRODUCTION

Have you ever asked yourself why do I find myself repeating the same old things? Why do I end up going through the same predicaments? Why can't I go any further in life, or why can't I be prosperous like other people? When will I ever get my breakthrough in life? Why does it feel like my life is going in circles and why do I keep ending up back in the same place I started?

Why is there so much separation in my family? Why can't we all get along? Why won't we help one another? Why are we still doing the same things? Why are our children growing up doing the same things that we are doing?

People are asking these questions every day. All over the world people and families are living their lives chained and bound. It is alarming because they do not know it. People are suffering and their lives are being destroyed because they do not understand the cause of their failures. Many have given up on being successful and blame others for it. Families are being affected in many ways. Many are faced with a **CURSE.** This curse disguises itself with many names: fear, failure, greed, etc. The unlearned will not identify it as a curse.

It is an ongoing cycle that repeats through families. Many are defeated because they lack the knowledge of this curse. It is basically being transferred to generation after generation. It is a GENERATIONAL CURSE. It is time for people to open their eyes and stop living their lives in defeat.

I once felt like giving up until I realized there was more to life than what I thought. How could I tell the world from the walls of prison? How could I give people something that could change their lives forever? Then my answer came. Write a book. Faced with fear, doubt, and past failures, I sit here today writing this book to the world, hoping to be effective in a positive way.

# Chapter 1

## DESCRIBING THE CURSE

Have you ever had someone call you bad names or say hurtful things about you? Did the words stick with you for years and have a negative impact on your life? Did that person's words give you a sense of fear to the point of being held back? Did you feel like it had a hold on you and you could not accomplish things in life?

Have you ever had a bad experience in your life? Did it have such an impact on you that you could not get it out of your mind? Did this experience cause you to fear doing things that could possibly benefit you? Did it have a long term impact on your life and cause you to dissociate yourself from things and people out of fear.

A curse can impact someone for years. A curse can be described as something that is *inflicted* or *afflicted* with harm or misery. It can have a long lasting negative effect. A curse can occur through words or an event. A curse can cause great damage in your life. It can cause stagnation if not recognized and nothing is done about it. Curses have torn apart families.

What makes this curse **GENERATIONAL?** A generation is typically defined as twenty to thirty years. The reoccurrence of something to those who come after makes it a Generational event. Simply put, the event repeats itself throughout the years.

Here is an example in which a pattern of negative behavior is handed down and repeated. Take a child and his or her parents for example. The parents have not finished school, and most of their conversations are non-influential. They never encourage the child. This is not good for the child because he or she has the full potential of turning out like the parents. Because the child does not have the proper upbringing and positive influence, the child will probably grow up the same as the parents. The child will have inherited the curse through the parents. He or she will grow up doing what he or she knows how to do.

People need to know all of the dangers of falling under the curse. This cycle is destroying our children right before our eyes. It is tearing lives apart and causing so much misery. This cycle must be broken! You hold the power to break the generational curse in your family.

# Chapter 2

## THE LACK OF EDUCATION

There are millions who have dropped out of school only achieving a partial education. A lot of people would say that is all that you need to make it in life. You are selling yourself short if you think that. Why would you want to limit your knowledge? It is an excuse for those who do not want to evolve or become more successful. A lot of people settle for less when they do not have to. The potential is there, but that is all it is when we chose to be content with less. Whose fault is it that you cannot get a job in the corporate world? You cannot become a doctor, lawyer, police officer, or the President of a corporation without an education.

What you don't know can hurt you!

A lot of people have found themselves deprived of opportunities because of what they did not know. There are people who are very talented and have potential. However, not having an education leaves them disappointed. We are the ones to blame and no one else. We have to hold ourselves accountable for our own actions. There is a reason why people tell their children to stay in school. School provides some of the tools that are needed to do well as an adult.

I wanted to be a professional football player. I prevented myself from achieving that goal when I dropped out of school. I did not take advantage of the opportunity of preparing for the future. Life does not always turn out the way we would like, but we must give ourselves a chance at something better. When we don't, we are cursing ourselves. We set ourselves up for failure. All this does is prevent you from moving forward.

Children drop out of school and turn to the streets. Later they wonder how things could have been had they stayed in school and given themselves a chance. There is this saying, "What you don't know can't hurt you". That isn't true because it can hurt you. At some point in our lives, we have to be accountable for the choices that we make, however that choice affects you.

# THE BLAME GAME

We love to blame people for the choices we make. Why not? It is the easy way out. For some, it is the best way to explain how we have failed. For most of us, it is a cop-out. We cannot admit that we messed up so we blame others. A lot of us blame our parents. We blame them for how our lives turned out. It's true that a lot of us had a difficult childhood. Our parents had some issues. It may have had an effect on you, but you cannot blame them for everything!

We all have had some hurtful experiences and have been discouraged because of them, but how do we move forward? We have to stop allowing other people's situations to determine our future. Allowing another person to affect you can diminish your potential. You have to make the choice to advance.

# THE POTENTIAL

Every day we meet people with talent. The expectation for a satisfying future is there. It doesn't always happen. Why is that? People are sometimes impacted by tragedies, loss of a loved one, lack of finances, or simply being told that they cannot do something! People face these challenges every day. They have dreams and plans then something or someone comes along to distract them.

I had a friend that had so much potential. I knew he would one day become successful at whatever he chose, but it was all taken away from him over time. He experienced abuse and neglect from his family. His father was not involved in his life. His mother was on drugs. He loved to play basketball and was very good at it. He was very smart. He even got good grades in school. He would always come up with ideas to make money.

His mother would always yell at him. She told him that he was going to be just like his good for nothing father! I never heard his mother say anything positive to him. She never hugged him. Eventually the verbal abuse became physical. He ran away from home. He never returned to school. The next time I saw him, he was selling drugs and later he was incarcerated. He had plenty of potential but he was robbed of it. He was not given the chance to flourish.

Potential means to have or show the capacity to develop into actuality. I had friends who went to college, but they did not do anything with their education. They were smart, intelligent people with bright futures. Why did they stop pursuing their goals? They allowed drugs and other pressures to discourage them.

Knowledge is power. If you don't use the knowledge you have, you may become powerless. When you allow negative people and influences to enter your life that slowly erodes your power. Every day there are struggles, and temptations. You have to overcome those things or they will consume you. You will find yourself making excuses for everything. You don't need negativity in your life.

You need people around you that are going to encourage you to do the right things. When times get hard, you need someone to tell you that you can make it. People stop pursuing goals because pressures overwhelm them. People make excuses all the time. They say things like; my parents did not make it either, so I guess I will end up the same way. They are only cursing themselves with discouragement, fear of failure, and doubt. They need to break the cycle and continue forward. Change the outcome to what you want it to be. The power is inside you. Never give up on yourself. We are faced with struggles every day, but that does not mean we should limit ourselves or give up.

# NO RESPECT OF PERSON

A tragedy could happen to anyone. A child, the college student, the business person, it doesn't matter who! The fact is everyday lives are being affected. No matter if your young or old; rich or poor, it doesn't matter. We see it every day in the lives of others as well. You have seen this curse take place in someone's life. Just as I have seen it and experienced it myself. The moment that I decided to stop attending school, and started hanging in the streets, is when I opened the door, for something that changed my life for the worse.

Drugs are a curse, and they destroy lives. How can a child fend for himself? He cannot. What about the college student? He can be on the right path until pressures begin to build. This makes it hard for him to study. His grades are affected. He may become depressed. He may turn to drugs to take his mind off his problems.

It is up to you whether you succeed or fail. No one ever said that life would be easy. You are going to have some challenges in life. It is up to you how you handle obstacles. We are sometimes met with trials in life that can either build us up, or it can tear us down. Challenges can be a stepping stone in life or they can destroy you.

## Chapter 3

## NO ONE SAID IT WOULD BE EASY

Life comes with struggles, whether you are rich or poor, white or black. A lot of us go through some intense situations, but it does not mean that we should quit! Some people see struggles as a bad a thing. That is not always true. There are people who will tell you that they appreciate the struggles that they have faced. How can someone appreciate struggle? Well, the situation can cause you to see things differently. It can have a positive impact. They have survived. Perseverance does something to our character. We push through difficulties and find strength. We learn to appreciate the things that we have been through because in some way it causes us to grow.

I remember a situation that happened to my family. It had a powerful effect on me. I believe that I later benefited from it. I can appreciate it because it taught me not to surrender. I was twelve or thirteen years old. My younger brother and sister were still infants. My mom was a single parent at the time. She had difficulties providing for the family. She struggled to keep food on the table and clothes on our backs.

I remember my mom saying, "I need help". It was just too much for her to do alone. I hated seeing my mom stress about the bills. It angered me. I told my mom that I would get a job to help. I went out with my shovel going from door to door asking my neighbors if they wanted their snow shoveled. My mom was not aware that I was doing this. She thought I was outside playing with friends. In one day I made fifty dollars. I gave it to my mom. I recall the look on my mom's face when I gave her that money. She smiled at me and said, "Where did you get this money? "

I told her I earned it shoveling snow. She looked at me with amazement. I knew she was okay with it when she hugged me and told me be careful. It really made me feel good to be able to help out my mom. Just to see her smile was great, but I knew that wasn't enough and I had to do more. I got a paper route.

My mom received a call from the paper station manager verifying that I was applying for a paper route. I was standing with him when he made the call. Then he passed me the phone. My mom said, "What are you doing Lamont?" I said, "Mom you said you need help with things, so I am trying to help". She told me to give the phone back to the manager and come home. I thought for sure that I was in trouble.

I passed him the phone and he spoke with her for a few moments. He turned to me and shook my hand, and said, "Welcome aboard Mr. Williams. I will give you a schedule next week. You are hired." Of course, when I got home my mother gave me the third degree. She was also proud of me because I stepped up to responsibility. It really felt good to help out my mom, but it also made things harder for me. There were times that I would come home from school and go straight to my paper route. I wasn't able to play with my friends and do all the fun things they did. It became boring quickly, but I was determined to help my family. It wasn't easy for me to do. I had to make sacrifices. I wanted to be like other twelve and thirteen year olds. I realize now that going through that helped me develop in certain areas of my life.

My struggles helped me build character. I learned how to be responsible. I always kept a job. I was determined to go after things of importance to me. No one said life would be easy. It comes with struggles and trials. It can make you or break you. Don't give up on your ideas and dreams. Don't live your life chained and bound by the curse. When things become difficult, remember to keep pushing. We all have the potential for greatness.

Sometimes we have to reach deep down within ourselves, and find what motivates us. In my case, it was seeing my mother struggle. I hated to see my mother like that. It sparked something within me to find a way to help her. Looking back, things were very difficult for us, but we managed to survive. My experiences taught me determination. It could have been too much for me. I could have quit my job and went back to playing with my friends, but this was my priority.

Life in a lot of ways is very similar to taking a test. It is just like school, if you pass the test you move forward. If not, go back and study until you are ready. We should learn from our experiences. Things happen so that we can learn from them. One test comes, then another one. It may not be as hard as the last one, or it may be harder. It's not always easy nor is it always hard, but experience is the best teacher!

# Chapter 4

# EVOLVING IN LIFE

One of the reasons families are finding themselves in the same place doing the same old stuff, is that they never evolve. They do not put themselves in a position to evolve. For example, when you drop out of school, you hinder yourself from education. You limit your knowledge. Whether we want to admit it or not, this is self inflicted. We sit there not doing anything to take us further in life. You just can't go with the flow of the world. It gets you nowhere.

You watch other people become successful. Why can't you have the same things they have or more? You don't have the necessary tools. You are not in the position to do the things you would like. You are complacent and confined to your lifestyle. We have to come up from under the curse. It is destroying our lives, and we are not the only ones being affected by it. It damages our children and families too.

How are you going to help your child with her home work if you don't have a education? A family is only strong as its leader. We wonder why children are not getting a proper upbringing or a proper education. A lot of that falls back on the parents. The decisions we make affect the child also.

## ONLY DOING WHAT THEY KNOW

People rarely step outside what they know. They become satisfied with their way of living. They limit themselves to doing things that are within their comfort zone. They won't do what it takes to get things done. They look for shortcuts or have someone else to do things for them. They settle for a temporary fix only to find themselves back in the same position again. They never step out of the box but they are quick to believe any dream that someone sells them, without investigating it first.

I can recall trying to give some family members some very valid information on purchasing a house. The information that I gave them required a little research, and it would have been a lot cheaper for them, but they decided that the information that I was giving them was too good to be true. They did not even take the time to research the information. They decided to take the advice of a crooked real estate agent who sold them a dream. He told them what they wanted to hear and they bought in to it hook, line, and sinker. Later they found out that the house had an outstanding payment on the mortgage.

They wound up in serious debt. They eventually lost the house because they could not afford to pay the mortgage. It could have been avoided had they done the proper research. They ended up right back where they started with more debt. I wondered why they continued to put themselves in this type of situation. They had been in this position before.

It upset me to see people I loved make unhealthy decisions. I came to understand they were only doing what they knew. This is how the curse operates. People find themselves repeating the same behavior over and over again.

I have a relative a lot of people would call a hustler. The problem is that his hustle is not a hustle at all. He uses people to get what he wants. He destroys lives with the things that he does. He knows how to get money, but in the wrong way. Surprisingly, he sometimes helps people with the money he gets but that has an ulterior motive. Every time that I hear about him or even speak to him, it is the same old stuff. The same old lifestyle. He uses people. He is a con artist. He lies to get what he wants. In his mind, it is okay to do these things because he has lived this way for so long.

When I say only doing what they know: It is not to say that they're evil and they only do bad things. Of course not, it just says that they only do what they have been taught. It does not mean that you are a bad person or a good person. It all boils down to you only operate with where you are in life. If you never progress to move forward in life that is where you stop. It is just like when you go through school as I demonstrated earlier. When you go through school you graduate from that grade then you pass to the next. You have learned at that level so you move on to the next level. Now let's say that you drop out of school after you have completed the eighth grade. Then that is where your progression of education stops. It's not common to achieve your goals with a ninth or tenth grade education. I'm not saying it's impossible, but because you didn't get enough education at those levels it may stop your progress! People do not understand the severity in how this affects their lives. You go through life being held back from achievement and success because of what you do not know, and all that means is that you have not met the necessary requirements to expand your ability to learn in life. So you go through life only doing the things that you know.

# THE LIFE STYLE

The life you live can affect and determine the future. Negative and positive cannot go together. It is either one or the other. Just like oil and water they do not mix. Like a young person trying to hang out in the streets with a bad crowd, and wonder why they're getting bad grades in school. How about the working person who spends their time smoking drugs only to find themselves fired from their job. How about the athlete with the gambling problem, who whines up losing their home, cars, and even their family, these are the kinds of things that can set you up for failure, you can be on the right path to success, but if you allow negative things into your life, it can quickly take a detour for the worse.

I can remember a relative who found himself in this situation. He did not have an education, but he was always a hard worker at his job. He was married, and had children; I would say that he was doing quite well for himself. One thing that I knew for sure about him was that he loved to gamble. One day his gambling caught up to him in a very bad way. His gambling became an addiction. He would use the money for bills and go gamble it way. He found himself begging other people for money, so that he could support his gambling addiction.

In the end he lost his family. His wife could not take it anymore because it was damaging their lives. She took their children and left him. My relative's curse was his addiction to gambling. He lost everything because he chose to live a lifestyle that cost him everything that he loved and cared for. His curse was no different from any other. He was not the only one hurt in this situation; his family was damaged as well.

The curse can come at you from many directions. For example, the young person who drops out of school and decides to sell drugs. He becomes a drug dealer and makes lots of money selling drugs. He does this for several years. He buys a house and a few cars. Things are going well, until he gets arrested. He is only doing what he knows, but the lifestyle that he lives will lead to prison or death.

Ultimately, nothing good can come from living that way. This is the self inflicted curse, because he chose that life knowing what it was.

We all have made choices in our lives that we are not necessarily happy with. Some of us live with regret. We look back and we wish that we could take it back and start all over again. What would cause us to regret the choices that we made? Could it be the heartache, and wasted time? Have you ever said to yourself, "If I would've done this ten years ago, I wouldn't be in the situation that I'm in today?" "Had I known back then that the decisions I made would have had an effect on my life today, I would've never made those choices."

Life comes at us from all angles with all sorts of things that we do not understand. Some of us learn from our experiences quicker than others. It may take some of us a short period to get it. For others it may take a life time. Life takes us through ups and downs, hills and valleys. We are met with obstacles where we have to make critical decisions. A life changing moment can come at us when things are difficult. You may feel pressure. This decision will help determine your future. Whatever you are going through at that time can either make you or break you. You can hang your head low in defeat or you can lift your head high.

Some of us convince ourselves that we are doing the right things with some of the decisions that we make. We are not thinking about the effect it could have on us. We think selfishly, not considering the ones that we love can also suffer from the choices that we make. We seek temporary satisfaction. We do not understand that it will change our lives forever.

# FEAR OF STEPPING OUT OF THE BOX

One of the ways of recognizing this curse is that it holds you back. It uses things like pain, fear, hate, and bad experiences that may have happened against you. It holds you back from achieving. Some people have been held back for so long that they find themselves in a box. A box is meant to hold things in and keep them secure. We live our lives in a box. We fear stepping out the box. We are afraid to try something different because we fear we will fail.

People have been held back because of past pain. Some people have been in a box for so long that they are satisfied with being there. I see women who suffer from this a lot. Some women stay in relationships with a man who cheats or is abusive. They go on to the next relationship and that man does something to her that puts her in shut down mode. When she meets a potentially good man, he does not have a chance with her. She feels every man is out to do her harm. Some women have gone for years without having a relationship because they have been scarred from being hurt repeatedly.

When a good man comes into her life, she pushes him away. She won't allow him to show her the other side of things. She has never had a good man so she does not know how it feels to have one. She may have seen it in someone else's relationship, or even desired to have what they have, but she can never allow it because of fear. She is trapped in a box of pain and hurt. The love of her life could be staring her right in the face, but she will never get the chance to experience it because she has a wall up. How can a person want something but push away what they are longing for? That is what happens when your heart is damaged.

Someone once told me that if you hold onto what a person has done to you, that person has power over you. For a while I did not get it. Then I experienced it for myself. Anything that remotely relates to the experience makes you think of them and what they have done.

You are holding on to the past. Forgive but don't forget. We forgive so that we can move on with our lives and be at peace with ourselves. We don't forget. We can learn from these experiences. We become better equipped for situations that may come in the future.

There are times when we feel that we are at fault for the decisions that others make. For example, something may have happened to someone that you cared about and you felt as though it would have never happened if you were there. People carry this pain all the time. They won't do things that could possibly be beneficial for them because they are afraid of stepping outside of the box. We have to stop living our lives in fear. At some point, we have to move forward.

When we hold onto things we create more pain for ourselves. You cannot hold yourself responsible for what you don't have control over. Forgive yourself. Tell yourself that I am not going to let anything or anyone hold me back anymore. It is not easy to overcome, especially when it is someone that you love and care about. It does not always heal easily. It takes time.

# Chapter 5

## MY LIFE EXPERIENCES

Looking back on my life, I can remember living under the curse. I remember my family suffering as well. Growing up I always went to school. I got good grades. At one point school was fun and I looked forward to going every day. I was always involved with school functions like plays, concerts, and things. I was liked by a lot of my teachers and they made sure that I did well also. I can remember getting promoted to the honors class. My teachers felt that I was smart enough after they saw the work that I had done.

I do not know what happened but I felt as though I could not do it anymore. It was simply too hard for me. Everyone wanted to see me do well so they pushed me with the work. I believe that they pushed me a little too hard because I had gotten very discouraged with my school work. They decided to put me back in my regular grade.

I can remember going from school to school because my mom was always moving. I remember having to watch my little brother and sister. When I wanted to play with my friends or spend the night over a relative's house, I could not. I would have to stay home so that I could watch my younger brother and sister. Things were not always fun for me when I was younger. As I got older things began to get harder.

I use to think that my mom was being very mean to me, but she was just trying to protect me from being around certain things. Other times I believed that she was being selfish. I became rebellious. I would skip school and hang out with friends. My grades began to reflect my absences. When my grades began to drop, my mom put me on punishment. I believe she was only able to discipline me so much because my dad was not really around. He had his own life and I was not really a part of it. My mom tried to do his part as best as she could. Not having my dad around much played a major role in my life. Instead, I was around my uncles who sadly did a poor job as role models.

I picked up some of their bad habits. I started doing some of the things that I saw them do. However, my mother stayed on me about school. By the time I reached high school, things began to take a turn for the worse. I was going to school and I was working at Farmer Jacks grocery store. It was hard, but I seemed to be doing fine. There was so much pressure on me. I would come home from school, change clothes, and leave for work. I remember being very tired when I came home at night, only to get back up in the morning and go to school. I barely had time to do my homework. I really didn't have time for anything else except on the weekends. Then I would get called in to work and I was not going to turn it down because I really enjoyed my job.

I got paid every Friday. It allowed me to get some of the things I wanted and help my mom out with things. I found myself working a lot of overtime. I even got a promotion which demanded more work hours for me. I really felt good. I was making money on my own. I was being responsible until my grades began to drop again. School became secondary to me. I missed more and more days.

One day my mom and I got into a very heated argument. My school called my mom explaining that my grades had dropped. They told her I was missing too many days of school. I had to go to summer school so I could pass to the next grade.

I allowed other things to come into my life. I began to hang out more with my friends. I went to parties. Income tax time rolled around and I received a nice refund. I told my mom that I was going to buy a car. Getting a car meant that I could get around better, but it also meant more responsibilities. My mom and I had another heated argument about what kind of car I should purchase. I ignored her advice. Instead, I took the advice of someone else and bought a car that I could not afford. My mom was upset with me. She was very disappointed that I did not listen to her. That was just the beginning of things to come. Hanging out with friends took the place of school. I dropped out of school in the tenth grade. I tried to go back but I had missed too many days.

I was never at home anymore. My mom was losing her grip on me. One day she asked me to watch my sister and brother while she went out with her friends. I told her no because I had to work that night. Everything seemed to be unraveling in my life. I began to smoke weed, drink alcohol, mess with a lot of females, and go to clubs. I was spending time with people that had a negative influence on me. The curse was beginning to take a toll on my life. I enrolled to get my GED. There were too many distractions in my life. My instructor tried to convince me to stay in school, but eventually I quit going. Things became worse. I was hanging out so much that I would be late for work. I was transferred to another store, with a warning that the next time I would be fired.

My life went quickly downhill. The more I hung out, the more I drank and smoked weed. The street life was changing who I truly was. I knew I should not be doing these things. I was impressionable and wanted to fit in with everyone else. I knew better, but I chose to block it out. I allowed my surroundings to dictate my actions. I began to stay the night away from home. I would be exhausted from a long day at work and still party into the morning hours. This took a toll on my body as well.

I spent time with people who sold drugs. I had fights at the club. it seemed like trouble found me everywhere I went. I eventually lost my job. My income was gone. I had a car note which I could not pay. I struggled to keep gas in my car. My car was repossessed. I had to hear "I told you so" from my mom.

Everything had changed. I dropped out of school. I lost my job. I lost my car. I was very focused at one point. Something made things unravel in my life. I took a wrong turn somewhere along the line.

My mom said to me one night, "I had a bad dream about you getting into fights going to those clubs. Maybe you should stop going out so much." I had never told her about any of the fights that I had at the clubs. I did not take heed to anything that she told me. The next time that I went out to the club, me and some of the guys that I hung out with, were thrown out of the club for fighting. We could not return.

The next time, we went to a different club, only to find ourselves in another fight. We left that night driving around talking about what happened. It was all fun and laughs because we all came out okay. I thought about what my mom said.

I hung out with my cousin a lot. Most of the time, we would be together during those club fights. He and I were very close at the time. One night he said to me, "We can't keep going to clubs and getting into fights because that is not us". I agreed with him. We decided that we would start going to more sophisticated places with an older crowd.

I often found myself broke and frustrated. There were times that I would be on my knees crying to God asking him "What happened? Why was everything going wrong for me?" I never heard anything back. I would just sit there on my knees silently looking up at the ceiling. Sometimes I didn't think God was listening. The more that I called out for Him, the more it appeared He was not listening to me.

There were times that I wanted to end my life. I fought every day to stay strong. I hoped that something would change soon. Something was about to change, but for the worse. I was arrested for murder in the first degree. All I remember was I was approached by a devil in the form of a man. He offered a group of us a job. The job required us to rob a person. We would get $1000 each. However, his plan was to kill the person. He manipulated the situation. I was charged with murder. I was left holding the bag.

It felt like a ton of bricks had hit me. I sat in the county jail. It all happened so fast. When I called home all my mom did was cry. I spoke with my grandmother and it was the very first time that I had ever heard her cry. My younger brother and sister were crying because they missed their brother. What was I going to do?

I came to the realization, that I hurt a lot of people by putting myself in this position. They cried as though I had died. How could I have been so selfish? I wanted to change things, but it was too late. I had finally hit rock bottom. I was tried and convicted in court. I was sentenced to life in prison, without a chance of parole.

# IDENTIFYING THE CURSE

What brought me to this point? How did I get off the path of success? What did I allow in my life to send me to prison? As I look back, I can see where I went wrong. I have no one to blame but myself. I made those choices. A lot of those choices were not good ones. Of course, there were some things that were beyond my control. I was missing something in my life. My mom did her best trying to raise me. She could have done some things differently. There's a possibility that it would have made a difference in how I handled things. In the end, I made those choices to put me in this position.

My father's lack of involvement played a part too. He was in and out of my life. There are things that a mother cannot give a child that a father can. There are certain things that a father cannot give a child that a mother can. My mother tried to fill the father role, but she was not my father.

Dropping out of school really played a major part in my journey to prison. Partying and the street life were more exciting to me than school. I was having fun. The streets became my teacher. I would smoke weed and drink alcohol just to escape the pressures that I was facing. It only made things worse. When I had those things in my system I used poor judgment. I allowed temptations into my life.

I associated with the wrong crowd. People that did not have my best interest. People that were a bad influence on me. If you hang out with people who do nothing but party, fight, smoke drugs, and drink alcohol, what do you expect to happen? Was I going to stay in school, and continue to work? Of course not! You cannot live two lives. There are blessings and there are curses in this world. There is life and there is death. You have to choose.

People who are a negative influence are not your friends. They will drag you down if you hang around them. The things that they do will rub off on you. You will find yourself doing the same things they are doing. That is what happened to me. I followed the wrong crowd. I picked up their habits. It caused a negative impact on my life. I dropped out of school. I lost my job. I ended up in prison.

That was my curse. There are a lot of people that can relate to my situation in some form or fashion. This thing caused a lot of damage in my life. It also caused me to hurt people that I care about and love. Can I recover from this curse? If I can, how do I break it?

# BREAKING THE CURSE

I was in the county jail on my way to prison. In the county jail, you get a lot of time to think. I don't think I ever did that much thinking in my life. I can remember the lonely nights lying there wondering what happened to my life. There were times that I thought I was dreaming. Then reality set in that this was all real. I was sentenced to life in prison. I found myself doing some very heavy thinking. I thought in ways that I had never thought. My mind was working so hard, and I became so depressed and stressed out, that it actually made me sick.

One day I decided to go to church service on another floor. I listened to the minister speak. He explained things about the bible that I never understood. At the end of the service the minister gave an invitation to anyone who wanted to accept Christ in their life. I came from a Christian background, but I never truly lived that life. There was a great tug at my heart. I stood up that day and I gave my life to Christ Jesus. I read my bible every day. I prayed a lot.

My mom came to visit. I was so happy to see her. She told me that I was glowing and there was a peace over me. I told her that I was saved now. I had given my life to the lord. She told me to memorize Psalm 91:1-16. I read it every day until it was in my heart. Most guys that go into prison turn towards some religion. People that hit rock bottom call out to God because they realize that they need help. This is where He got my attention. I now had a relationship with the Father, but this was just the beginning for me.

It was time for me to go upstate. I had a long road ahead of me. The way I looked at life all began to change. I was going to have to make some major decisions. I began to watch and learn. I knew that it was not going to be easy. I was determined not to let this situation dictate my life. I decided that it had to start there with my mind. I had to change my way of thinking.

# Chapter 6

## TRANSFORMATION OF THE MIND

As I began to see some of the things that others were getting into, I began to see myself in a lot of those guys. I would listen to some of their conversations, and wonder if I talked like that. Over time, some of the things that were said and done angered me. I was not going to be like that. I didn't judge anyone, because once I did those same things. All I knew was I did not want this life. I wanted better for myself.

I decided that I was not going to be miserable. I wanted peace of mind. I did not want to be stuck in that lifestyle. I was not about to give up on life. At times, I would be hard pressed on every side with the things that went on around me. I was not the only one going through this. My family suffered because of my decisions and they were hurt too. I owed it to myself, but I also owed it to my family.

I began to read more. I went to school and focused on getting my GED. That was something that I really wanted to accomplish. I studied hard. I concentrated on what was important. Things became a lot clearer to me. I began to see and understand things so differently. I even learned things about myself that I never knew. I had a job working in the barbershop. I was good at cutting hair. I never thought that I would be a barber, but it was fun and I enjoyed it. We had a lot of laughs in the barbershop. I also had some serious times, where I found myself giving advice and encouragement. I also received it.

I received my GED and it was a great feeling. I rarely accomplished anything before then, but I now had a whole new outlook on life. I wanted more. More changes occurred in different areas of my life. I was maturing in my thinking. I quit doing things that were not healthy for me, like hanging around the wrong group of guys. I decided that I would be my own man. I was not going to allow others to have a negative influence on me anymore. I thought that I could be a positive influence on others.

I made better decisions. I stopped trying to be accepted by others. I even quit using foul language. People began to respect me. Not because I demanded it, but they saw something new in me. It really felt good making these changes. It felt like a weight was being lifted off me. I did not understand that I was beginning to break the curse.

The changes drove me to get more involved with other things like, self help classes, learning social skills, and motivational classes. I found a great liking for these things. They were missing from my life. I had the joy of learning back, and it was even better than before. As I dealt with the struggles of being locked up, it brought me closer to the Lord. I found peace that enabled me to cope with my situation. When I could not reach out to family for love, the Lord was always there to comfort me. I prayed and read my bible more. Life can sometimes be very confusing but the bible made it all so much clearer for me.

In the beginning, I thought that I was going to have to be some religious fanatic. It was not like that at all. I had a relationship with the Lord. That allowed me to have balance in my life. I was able communicate better and even help someone else in need. I had learned that it was not just about me. It was about serving someone in need. I was not the only one with needs.

When I think about it, I had plenty of warnings when I was out running the streets. My mom had those dreams for a reason. I was being warned to stop what I was doing. You only get so many warnings before something happens that you later regret.

I regret that I did not listen to advice from people that could have possibly detoured me from coming to prison. I believe everything happens for a reason. This may have been the only way for me to get it. It may have been in His plan because I could have lost my life if I continued doing the things that I did. I hate that it took this, in order for me to change. At the same time, I am so grateful because it saved my life. This curse could have broken me, but I survived. I had a better way of living.

I opened my eyes to new things. I noticed things that were there all the time. I could not see them because I was blinded by the curse. It kept me from seeing what was right in front of me. I could not see the truth. It had an effect on my thinking. It caused me to make poor decisions.

This curse had my life in chains. I was trapped by it. I was finally breaking its hold on my life. It was no longer tearing my life apart. It was a relief, a breath of fresh air. I began to apply myself and accomplish things. It felt good to do so. I set goals for myself. If there were things that I did not know, I would ask someone for help. I was not afraid. I wasn't ashamed anymore. I was breaking down walls. Even though I was locked up in prison, I was free!

# Chapter 7

# Breaking Free

I was now mentally free. I was also spiritually free from the things that once held me back. My eyes were open. My mind was no longer cloudy.

Being in prison has a way of bringing you down. You are confined and away from the people you love and care about. Prison has impacted people to the point that they gave up on life. Prison will tear you down if you allow it to. Most prisoners only think about getting out. After a while it becomes depressive to the mind.

I would always think about going home. I would sometimes feel depressed. I missed my freedom. I asked myself would I go back to doing some of the things that I was doing before I got locked up. That was my moment of truth. I knew a lot of guys who got out of prison and do the same things that got them incarcerated in the first place. That is not what I wanted for myself. I decided I wanted a good life for myself. I asked some of the younger guys how can you be free if your mind is in bondage. They did not understand what I was asking them. Some of us feel that there is nothing wrong with our thinking. We are accustomed to the way things are.

When you have been in bondage for so long, you begin to accept it. You begin to believe that the things are okay, when they are not. When someone comes along and tells you things can be different, you get angry with them. I used to be that way. I realize that my way was not the right way. Unfortunately, I had to learn the hard way. When I decided that I wanted to change, I had to accept the knowledge that people offered me. I began detaching myself from the chains that held me down.

Your state of mind determines whether you are free or in bondage. You can be physically free and be mentally in prison. You can be physically in prison and mentally free. I know a lot of people that are free on the streets but living their lives in chains. I also know the people that are incarcerated but they are free. They are free from the curse that held them back for so long. The curse is a lot like prison. It keeps you from achieving anything. It limits you because it keeps your mind chained with doubt and fear.

As I continued to mature in my new found freedom, I noticed I was a lot happier. I could be still long enough to process things. I was moving too fast before and I did not know where I was headed. Now I know in which direction I want to go. I understand that it takes hard work. I know that I have to be persistent in order to reach my goals.

# REACHING BACK

Things began to change in my life. I was doing things to better myself and to make my situation better. I was much more appreciative of things and I was more understanding to what others were going through. I was more open minded. I noticed others began to ask me for advice. I found myself wanting to help them. I wondered if this was my calling in life. I actually enjoy assisting people with their problems.

I was a positive person to be around. One day this guy that I barely knew asked me if he could speak to me about a problem that he had. He shared something with me that I thought he would share with someone he was closer to and could confide in. When I asked him why he chose to share it with me, he said he felt I was loyal. He also said he knew I would give him the truth. I told him that I would try to help him to the best of my ability.

More and more I found people would come to me for advice. I dealt with real life situations in which their lives depended. I did not and do not know the answer to everything but they would always appreciate me for whatever advice that I did give them. I did not advertise for people to talk to me but my conduct spoke for me. People were drawn to me by that alone.

I wanted to reach back and help others that I saw chained in some way or form. I involved myself in things that would enable me to help others. I took motivational and life skills classes. These classes helped me a great deal. I found out more about myself and started understanding things in life. Achieving those skills put me in a position to help someone else. I shared what I learned with those I thought would also benefit from it.

# Chapter 8

## THE NEW BEGINNING

It really felt good being able to help others as well as myself. Everything was new for me now. This was a new start at life. I was going down a different path. This path was narrow and I had no room for garbage. Now that my eyes were open, I was not going to allow the things that brought me down and held me captive to come into my life anymore. Why would I want to go back to that? I knew that more trials and struggles were in my future, but I would handle them differently now.

My mind was renewed. I had transformed my way of thinking. In the past, I did not want people to think that I was stupid. I would not ask questions. I learned when you don't ask, it can hurt you.

I know that things are not going to be easy. Life comes with struggles so that we can grow from them. Test, trials, and struggles prepare us for the future. It makes us stronger and better in different areas of our lives. You can either learn and benefit from your experiences or you can let them destroy you. I decided that I was going to fight for my life. It was not easy but with a lot of dedication and help from others, I was able to overcome many things.

Continuing my education was a great accomplishment for me but I did not stop there. I did other things that would help me too. I'm putting myself in positions for additional opportunities. I began to evolve in life. I became knowledgeable about more things. I began to approach situations with confidence. I was walking by faith, not fear. I was chasing success. I could taste it. My thinking was that I can do all things if I put my mind to it!

The light in me was now shining and nothing was going to put it out. Others saw the light in me through my walk, how I carried myself, my conversations, the way I talked, and my personality. I realized going through hard times had produced something greater in me. My character was different. I was more caring and more thoughtful towards others. I stopped selfishly thinking only about myself and my problems.

Although I was in prison physically, mentally I was free from those chains in my life. I was determined never to be bound again by them. I knew sooner or later my physical would catch up to my spiritual. I get on my knees when things overwhelm me. I look up and say Lord help me! He is the source of my strength. When I am weak, He gives me the strength to go on. When there is no one else to look to for encouragement, I have to encourage myself. I take a look around, and I see God's creation, and what He has done for me. That motivates me to keep going.

# Chapter 9

## THE NEXT GENERATION

Most people can identify with this curse. It has touched their lives and the people they love. Lots of people have suffered and families have been destroyed. Whether a terrible situation happened in your life, the life style you were living or just making poor choices, the fact remains that lives were hindered in many ways. People simply do not know what they are facing.

I do not expect for everyone to relate to what I have been through, but there is something that you may be dealing with and you have not found the solution to your problem. We are accustomed to seeing people suffer that we do not get the real picture. A lot of people will say that is the way life is. That may be true in many ways, but we are also talking about prevention. We can save someone from going through things that will have a negative impact on them. You can give them advice that could steer them in the right direction.

We see a generation of children growing up without the proper upbringing or with negative influences and we do nothing about it. They are exposed to so much that when they begin to rebel we say they are a lost cause. Our children are suffering. When a child grows up without his mother or father they are affected by it. If there is no structure or discipline in a child's life, he suffers. If the parents do not give the proper guidance the child suffers.

We have to take responsibility because our children are being lost to this curse. When our lives are in turmoil our children are affected as well. What we do has an effect on their future. Generation after generation is being afflicted and it is getting worse. We have to accept responsibility for our actions. It is time to step it up.

It is time to break this curse. It starts with us. What are you doing wrong? How can you be more effective in your child's life? If television is spending more time with your child than you are, put yourself in place of that television. Be more active in your child's life. You make the difference in their life. You prevent them from going down the wrong road by showing them love and holding them in your arms from time to time. Encourage them to do the right things.

Set your child up to have a bright future. Prepare them for the challenges that they will face and they will handle them. If you did not finish school, make sure that your child does. If drugs were your downfall and you recovered, make sure your child understands the importance of not allowing drugs into their lives. Their futures depend on it.

# CHANGING THE FUTURE

A lot of us can look back and see how our lives were greatly affected by the curse. If your life is in chains, you should want better for your children. They do not have to go through what you have been through. We need to change the pattern of this curse. We have to protect our children. Generations are being lost because they are not being protected. You can break this curse and change the future for your children.

For instance, if you have had an abusive life, show your children as much love as possible. Show them that you care. Ask them questions about what they like, find out what their interests are, love them in different ways, give them what you did not have, and you will change things. If you dropped out of school, show your child the importance of an education. Help them with their home work and be more involved with what they are doing. You play an intricate role in their lives point them in the right direction. Give them a chance at making better choices for themselves.

We can no longer sit back and watch this curse tear our families apart. We have to do something about it. Protect your future generations. If we just sit back and allow the curse to continue, we are just being selfish.

It all starts with the mind. That is what determines the road they will take in life. If their minds are filled with lots of negative things, it sets them up for failure. If their minds are influenced positively, they have a better chance at success.

We have taken our hands off and allowed the world to raise our children. We are allowing the world to influence their minds with unhealthy things. Our children are on the computer and we are not monitoring them. We wonder why they are being solicited by predators. Our children listen to music that encourages them to have a gun in their hands. They are watching inappropriate things on television. Know your child's friends. We can't always be there to hold their hands, but we must equip them with the necessary tools to help them guard against negative influences.

# Chapter 10

## TAKING BACK YOUR LIFE

We all have faced some tough challenges and some of us have been greatly affected by the situations we have gone through. You may have been in an abusive relationship, molested as a child, raped, or lost someone very close to your heart. Whatever you have gone through made you feel like you can't move forward with your life. It is time to take your life back. You have been defeated for too long. It is time for you to break the chains which have bound you for so long.

You can't let it rule your life anymore. If you have been holding on to something, let it go. If you don't release it you won't progress. If someone has wronged you, forgive them. Do not allow them to hold power over you. Don't let fear stop you from living your life to its full potential. You can't let hate, fear, doubt, and disappointment dictate how you are going to live your life. Stop telling yourself that you can't, because you can.

You are in control of your future. You can't let anyone dictate it for you. Break the chains in your life. Take your life back! Move forward and give yourself a chance at having healthy relationships. Try opening your heart to someone. Give them a chance to love you.

Some situations are a little more extreme than others so it may be harder to overcome or take longer to break the chain. Everything will not change overnight. It takes time. Take the time to think. Do not rush into anything. Use the time to heal and recover. Look at your situation with a better understanding. Then do something about it.

When we decide to do something about the situation that goes on in our lives, that's when we change our outlook on life itself. The way that you may think and feel about certain things that you are not educated enough to pursue may be the fact that you may need more education in that area. Most of the times we do nothing about this issue and it may hold us back from achieving things in life. When you can get away from that old negative and doubtful thinking then things can change for you. You can change the future for yourself and your family because it affects them too. Actions come next. People talk about what they want and never act on those things. They sit there and daydream about it. When you combine your words with actions things begin to happen. Do what is necessary to reach your goals. Your actions will strip the negativity of its power. You will find peace, love, and faith in your abilities. You can experience life at a different place. Put the curse under your feet! Be strong and live your life victorious! You can do whatever you set your mind to do.

When breaking these chains we have to replace the negative with positive. Create goals and go after them. Once you realize that you are free your outlook on everything changes. You are in control of your future. It all starts with the mind. However a man thinks so is he. If you are thinking negative that shall it be.

Stop making excuses or you will find yourself stuck in your current condition. If you think like a failure then that's what you'll be. If you are thinking success, then you are setting yourself up to be a successful person. Choose a healthier lifestyle.

Stop blaming others and take responsibility for not only yourself but someone else. Build someone up and tell them that they can make a change too. Motivate them to step outside of the box. Help them do what is necessary in order to reach their goal.

If you don't like where you are in life right now, stop complaining and do something about it. There is no one holding you back but yourself. If you don't know where to begin, start by telling yourself "I can do this!" Whatever you are struggling with, it is time to overcome it.

My eyes have been opened and the veil is off. I can help someone else with their struggles because it is no longer just about me. I have looked at myself and my surroundings. I have watched the things that happen. People's lives are being destroyed. They are chained in different ways. It disturbs my heart. This curse has touched so many lives.

Are you tired of living your life going in a circles, doing the same things over and over, making the same old choices? It doesn't have to continue. Stop the cycle of madness. Begin a journey towards success. Aim for prosperity. Know you and your children can live productive and fruitful lives. You don't have to be stuck in that same rut!

Change the condition of your thinking. Look around and look within yourself. The moment you decide that you want to change, you will now be on the right track. The next thing is to act on it.

Life comes at us in so many different ways. We don't understand why certain things happen to us. Just take life one day at a time and do your best.

# BREAKING THE GENERATIONAL CURSE

# MAKE

# A

# CHANGE

# TODAY

*Thank You  
Jesus for Everything*

# MOCY PUBLISHING, LLC
## BOOKS, EBOOKS, MUSIC & MORE!

This is a powerful book filled with information that describes how black people are failing to achieve their goals in life, personally, socially, spiritually, and financially. As well as highlighting the problems why black people are failing in life, this book will also describe the steps on how to correct the problems. If you would like to become a better achiever in life, read and understand the TWELVE REASONS WHY BLACK PEOPLE ARE LOSING IN LIFE.

Life is about change and knowledge is the key. So stop playing games with your life and receive the blessings God have in store for you. Tomorrow is a new day and by reading this book you'll find a new purpose for living.
*By Donele "Casino" Bailey*

**Price:** $14.99 (Paperback)
**Available:** September 11, 2012
**ISBN:** 978-0-9834700-0-7
**Item #:** MPB7165

Do you feel like you've been chained down all your life and something has been holding you back from your success in pursuing your dreams? Have you been affected by what someone have said or done to you, to the point of where you're unable to move forward with your life? Are you feeling held back in this world and no matter how much you try to move forward you end up back where you started?

**BREAKING THE GENERATIONAL CURSE** will show you how to break free from any curse in your life. This book will give you insight on how to overcome the past things that held you back in your life. This book will also allow you to overcome those struggles that we face in our everyday lives. You can take your life back and you don't have to be chained down anymore. Your change can start today! *By Lamont "Willy" Williams*

**Price:** $14.99 (Paperback)
**Available:** September 25, 2012
**ISBN:** 978-0-9834700-4-5
**Item #:** MPB7166

### Order Your Copy Now at
### www.mocypublishing.com
or Mail a Check or Money Order with order form below:

| QTY | ITEM # | DESCRIPTION | EACH | PRICE |
|---|---|---|---|---|
|  | MPB7165 | 12 Reasons Why Black People are Losing in Life | $14.99 |  |
|  | MPB7166 | Breaking The Generational Curse | $14.99 |  |
|  |  | Make Payable to:<br>Mocy Publishing, LLC<br>220 Bagley St. (Suite 1018)<br>Detroit, MI 48226-1400 | Shipping | $4.00 |
|  |  |  | Total |  |

www.ingramcontent.com/pod-product-compliance
Lightning Source LLC
LaVergne TN
LVHW051506070426
835507LV00022B/2959